Linux Firewall Gently -- Firewalld

Second Edition

Sujata Biswas

Content

The second edition of this book is a comprehensive guide to firewalld, the default firewall solution on CentOS 7 and other modern Linux distributions. It covers a wide range of topics, from setting up a simple firewall to configuring a multi-zone firewall with complex rules and policies.

This edition includes updated information on the latest features of firewalld, including setting up a multizone firewall and using XML configuration files. It also covers advanced topics such as using rich rules, direct rules, logging, and masquerading and NAT.

In addition, the book provides in-depth coverage of IP sets and how to use them with firewalld to create complex firewall rules. It also includes a detailed guide to fail2ban, a powerful tool for protecting your system against brute-force attacks and other types of malicious activity.

Whether you're a beginner looking to learn the basics of firewalld or an experienced administrator looking for advanced configuration options, this book has something for you. With clear, step-by-step instructions and real-world examples, you'll be able to implement a robust and effective firewall solution for your Linux system.

Prerequisites

If you're interested in learning about firewalld, a firewall management tool for Linux operating systems, it's important to have a basic understanding of networking concepts. While knowledge of the OSI model is not strictly necessary, it can be helpful in understanding how firewalld interacts with the network stack. However, the main focus of this book is on firewalld itself, and it will provide a thorough introduction to the tool, including installation, configuration, and management. By the end of this book, you'll have a solid foundation in firewalld and be able to secure your Linux system with confidence.

Firewalls are essential in protecting computers from viruses and information theft. As a personal user, a software firewall can suffice to protect against external dangers when connected to the internet. However, as an administrator, it is your responsibility to safeguard your servers, users, and data. Opting for a firewall hardware device, though more costly, can make more sense as it has more processing power and can check more incoming data, providing better protection for your devices. It's important to remember that even smartphones are now part of your network, so they should not be overlooked.

Think of a firewall as a barrier from the big bad world of the internet. It acts as a boundary wall that protects your home or office, allowing only legitimate individuals to gain access.

Firewalld, a firewall management tool for Linux operating systems, communicates with the Netfilter module in the Linux kernel using iptables. However, it does not use the iptables interface to communicate with Netfilter. Firewalld is managed using firewalld-cmd, a command line option. Netfilter empowers the Linux kernel to examine each data stream that comes into or goes out of a system. It is a module, a piece of code that is injected into the heart of the Linux operating system.

One of Firewalld's most significant advantages is that it is dynamic, meaning that the rules you write are instantaneously applied to the system without having to reload the daemon. A daemon is software that runs in the background.

Firewalld divides network traffic communications into zones for a system. For instance, the traffic that comes into your network from a user, such as Lucy, accessing her emails on the company's email server using her smartphone at the airport, encounters a different set of rules than a user like Jeff, who is inside your company's premises. Lucy is out in the big bad world using the internet, while Jeff's data is inside the company. Thus, the rules for Lucy's data are more stringent compared to Jeff's. From a security point of view, Lucy and Jeff, while working for the same company, are in different zones. The zone determines the level of trust, and Firewalld is responsible for managing the zones and their respective rules.

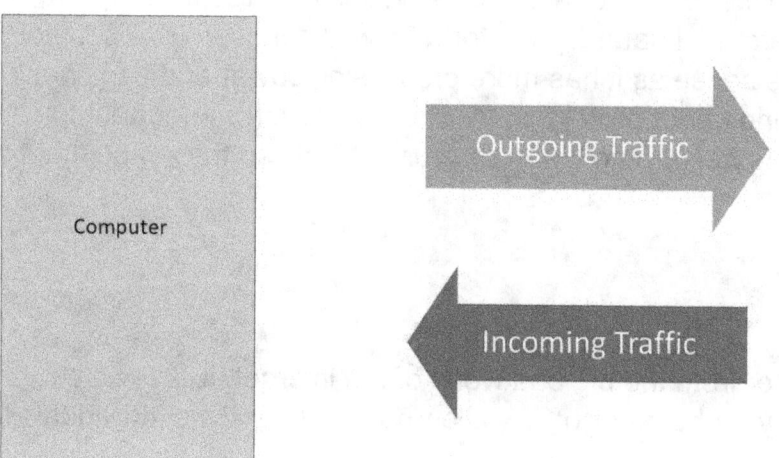

The diagram illustrates the difference between Outgoing and Incoming Traffic.

Outgoing Traffic: That which originates from your computer.

Incoming Traffic: The data stream which has your computer as the destination.

Firewalld is a Linux-based firewall management tool that provides a way to configure dynamic firewall rules in Linux systems. It replaces the older iptables firewall that was used in previous versions of Linux.

Here is a diagram that explains the basic architecture of Firewalld:

In Firewalld, the firewall rules are managed by zones. Each zone represents a specific level of trust for a network connection. For example, the "public" zone may have more restrictive rules than the "home" zone since it is considered less trusted.

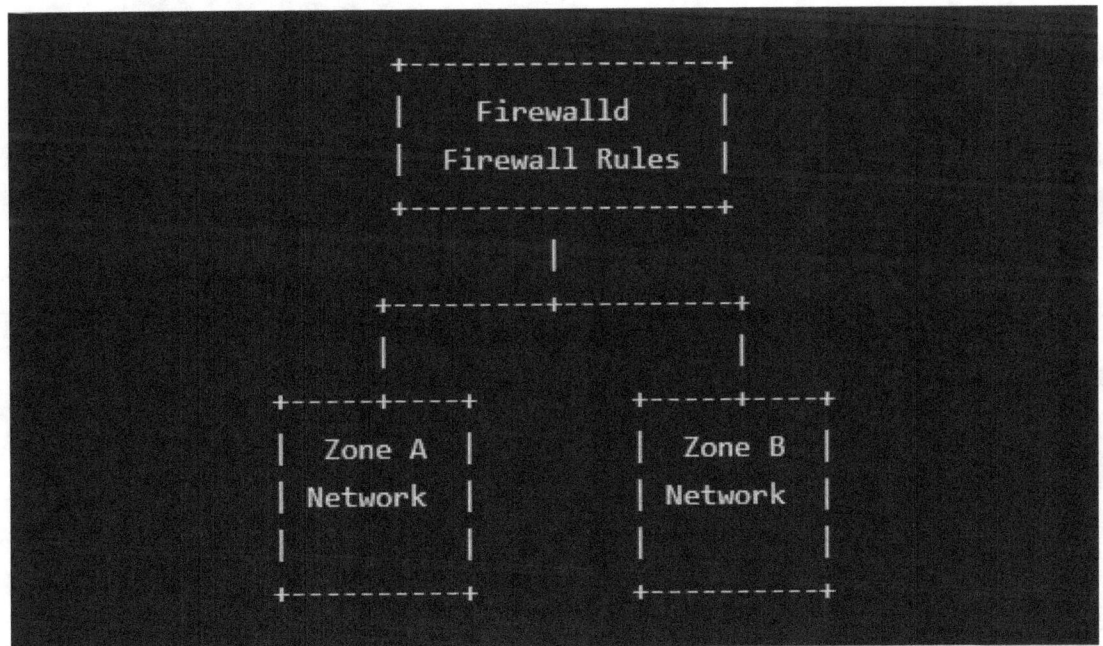

In the diagram, there are two zones: Zone A and Zone B. Each zone represents a network connection, such as a wired or wireless network. The networks in Zone A are considered more trusted than the networks in Zone B.

The firewall rules in Firewalld are applied at runtime, which means that they can be modified without requiring a system restart. This makes it easy to manage complex rulesets for different network connections.

Overall, Firewalld provides a flexible and easy-to-use firewall management tool for Linux systems.

There are 9 pre-defined Zones in the Firewalld depending upon the level of trust in ascending order. However, before you understand about zones, it is important to understand the difference between outgoing and incoming traffic, the following diagram illustrates the difference:

Zone Name	Level of Trust (Description)
Drop	This zone has the least level of trust and drops all incoming traffic without sending any acknowledgment to the sender. Allows all outgoing traffic.
Block	This zone is like the Drop zone, the incoming traffic is rejected, and the sender gets a message.
Public	Allows traffic from certain public networks depending upon the rules that you set.
External	Here the firewall is used as a gateway, and it represents the external interface to the world while keeping your internal network private.
Internal	The set of rules that apply to the computers in your private internal network.
DMZ	DMZ stands for Demilitarized Zones, an isolated patch of computers in your internal network that may not access to other internal resources. Imagine, a patient kept under isolation in case of disease breakout at the hospital
Work	This pertains to Work computers on your network, most services are allowed. The trust level is high.
Home	The trust level is higher than Work, most computers in this zone trust each other.
Trusted	The highest level, the most liberal and hence must be used with caution.

The first step in any system configuration is documentation. You may feel that you have everything under control, but after a few days you tend to forget the steps that you undertook to install the software.

Step 1:

Identify the Operating System using the following command

 # cat /etc/redhat-release

CentOS Linux release 7.4.1708 (Core)

Step 2:

Note the IP address and the hostname of the system, the command you use is **ip a** or **/sbin/ip a**

 # ip a

2: enp0s3: <BROADCAST,MULTICAST,UP,LOWER_UP> mtu 1500 qdisc pfifo_fast state UP qlen 1000

    link/ether 08:00:27:b5:aa:94 brd ff:ff:ff:ff:ff:ff

    inet 192.168.1.8/24 brd 192.168.1.255 scope global dynamic enp0s3

      valid_lft 253642sec preferred_lft 253642sec

    inet6 fe80::67fa:136:dd:fb4/64 scope link

      valid_lft forever preferred_lft forever

The IP address is 192.168.1.8

The hostname is found by using the **hostname** command:

 # hostname

bobby

Step 3:

Login as root.

Run the following command to install Firewalld:

 # yum install firewalld

.

.

.

Installed:

  firewalld.noarch 0:0.4.4.4-14.el7

Dependency Updated:

  firewalld-filesystem.noarch 0:0.4.4.4-14.el7

  python-firewall.noarch 0:0.4.4.4-14.el7

Complete!

Step 4:

Check if the Firewalld is installed using the **which** command:

 # which firewalld

/usr/sbin/firewalld

Step 5:

To automatic restart of the Firewalld daemon after restart/reboot using the **systemctl** command in the following manner:

 # systemctl enable firewalld

Step 6:

To check if the Firewalld is running on your system, use the **systemctl** command again:

 # systemctl status firewalld

• firewalld.service - firewalld - dynamic firewall daemon

  Loaded: loaded (/usr/lib/systemd/system/firewalld.service; enabled; vendor preset: enabled)

  Active: inactive (dead)

   Docs: man:firewalld(1)

As you can see it is dead, that is, not running.

Start the Firewalld by using the command:

 # systemctl start firewalld

Check the status again:

 # systemctl status firewalld

● firewalld.service - firewalld - dynamic firewall daemon

  Loaded: loaded (/usr/lib/systemd/system/firewalld.service; enabled; vendor preset: enabled)

  Active: active (running) since Sat 2018-09-08 21:54:58 IST; 2s ago

   Docs: man:firewalld(1)

 Main PID: 15541 (firewalld)

  CGroup: /system.slice/firewalld.service

       └─**15541 /usr/bin/python -Es /usr/sbin/firewalld --nofork --nopid**

Sep 08 21:54:58 bobby systemd[1]: Starting firewalld - dynamic firewall dae.....

Sep 08 21:54:58 bobby systemd[1]: Started firewalld - dynamic firewall daemon.

It is running.

There is another command you can use to see if the Firewalld daemon is running:

 # firewall-cmd --state

running

The response is running.

Let us explore the default zone, which you can find out by going listing the content of the directory **/etc/firewalld/zones**

 # ls -l /etc/firewalld/zones

total 8

-rw-r--r--. 1 root root 315 Feb 21 2018 public.xml

-rw-r--r--. 1 root root 315 Feb 21 2018 public.xml.old

As you can only configuration about the Public Zone is available. The correct way to check the default zone is by using the following command:

 # firewall-cmd --get-default-zone

public

The response is public, which we are already aware of.

To find the default rules associated with the public zone, enter the following command:

```
# firewall-cmd  --list-all
public (active)
  target: default
  icmp-block-inversion: no
  interfaces: enp0s3
  sources:
  services: ssh dhcpv6-client
  ports:
  protocols:
  masquerade: no
  forward-ports:
  source-ports:
  icmp-blocks:
  rich rules:
```

As you can see the services which are enabled are **ssh** (secure shell) and **dhcpv6-client**.

To see the rules in all the available zones, the command is

```
# firewall-cmd  --list-all-zones
```

The output of the above command is long.

You can enable a service to run in the public zone. From the previous section, we know that by default two services are allowed in the public (default) zone which are **ssh** and **dhcpv6-client**. Let's try and see we can allow another service in the public zone. To accomplish this task, you list down the services available on the system, which you can do by using the following command.

 # firewall-cmd --get-services

RH-Satellite-6 amanda-client amanda-k5-client bacula bacula-client bitcoin bitcoin-rpc bitcoin-testnet bitcoin-testnet-rpc ceph ceph-mon cfengine condor-collector ctdb dhcp dhcpv6 dhcpv6-client dns docker-registry dropbox-lansync elasticsearch freeipa-ldap freeipa-ldaps freeipa-replication freeipa-trust ftp ganglia-client ganglia-master high-availability http https imap imaps ipp ipp-client ipsec iscsi-target kadmin kerberos kibana klogin kpasswd kshell ldap ldaps libvirt libvirt-tls managesieve mdns mosh mountd ms-wbt mssql mysql nfs nfs3 nrpe ntp openvpn ovirt-imageio ovirt-storageconsole ovirt-vmconsole pmcd pmproxy pmwebapi pmwebapis pop3 pop3s postgresql privoxy proxy-dhcp ptp pulseaudio puppetmaster quassel radius rpc-bind rsh rsyncd samba samba-client sane sip sips smtp smtp-submission smtps snmp snmptrap spideroak-lansync squid ssh synergy syslog syslog-tls telnet tftp tftp-client tinc tor-socks transmission-client vdsm vnc-server wbem-https xmpp-bosh xmpp-client xmpp-local xmpp-server

The service we are interested to allow in the public zone is **telnet**. Now, mostly since **telnet** transmits data in clear text format, it is not allowed in the firewall rules, even explicitly. However, in fact, it is a nifty little tool that is often useful. Telnet provides text-based connectivity to the Linux/Unix/Solaris machines when you do not need GUI. You will learn to use telnet to troubleshoot Firewall issues.

Let us check if we can telnet from the Windows system to the Centos server whose IP address is 192.168.1.8.

Step 1:

Open a CMD window on your Windows 10 system.

Note: Telnet is NOT installed by default on Windows 10. You have to use "Turn Windows Features On or Off" to install Telnet client, only then you would have access to telnet on Windows 10.

```
C:\WINDOWS\system32\cmd.exe                                    —    □    ×

C:\>
C:\>telnet 192.168.1.8
Connecting To 192.168.1.8...Could not open connection to the host, on port 23: Con
nect failed
```

You get a cryptic message saying "Could not connection to the host, on port 23: Connect failed"

The telnet uses port 23 for communication, and since the service is not allowed by the Firewalld on Centos system, you cannot connect to the system using this port.

Step 2:

However, how do we know that telnet is failing due to the Firewalld? You must be sure. To be sure, you need to stop the Firewalld daemon in the Centos system and then check if telnet from Windows 10 to the Centos system is successful.

On the Centos system, **bobby**, shut the Firewalld daemon service using the following command:

systemctl stop firewalld

Check the status to be sure, using the following command:

systemctl status firewalld

● **firewalld.service - firewalld - dynamic firewall daemon**

   Loaded: loaded (/usr/lib/systemd/system/firewalld.service; enabled; vendor preset: enabled)

   Active: inactive (dead) since Sun 2018-09-09 00:39:04 IST; 2s ago

     Docs: man:firewalld(1)

   Process: 15886 ExecStart=/usr/sbin/firewalld --nofork --nopid $FIREWALLD_ARGS (code=exited, status=0/SUCCESS)

   Main PID: 15886 (code=exited, status=0/SUCCESS)

Sep 09 00:33:21 bobby systemd[1]: Starting firewalld - dynamic firewall daemon...

Sep 09 00:33:21 bobby systemd[1]: Started firewalld - dynamic firewall daemon.

Sep 09 00:39:04 bobby systemd[1]: Stopping firewalld - dynamic firewall daemon...

Sep 09 00:39:04 bobby systemd[1]: Stopped firewalld - dynamic firewall daemon.

Indeed, the Firewalld is down!

Step 3:

Let us check if the **telnet** command on Windows 10 is successful in opening a connection to the Centos system, **bobby**.

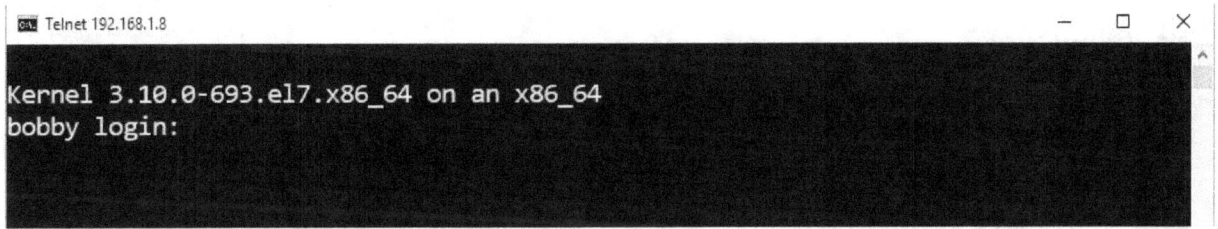

Yes, **telnet** is successful now. Proving that it is indeed the Firewalld that is not allowing the telnet connectivity to the Centos system, **bobby**.

You cannot, of course, have the system be without the firewall, you must add a rule in the Firewalld that allows the telnet service and consequently opens the port 23.

Step 4:

You know that the telnet service is available on the Centos system, to dig up information about this service, that is, view its XML file, you need to go to the **/usr/lib/firewalld/services** directory. This directory contains XML files relevant to each service.

Note: An XML (Extensible Markup Language) file is used to share information between various Internet/network entities.

```
# ls -l telnet*
```

-rw-r--r--. 1 root root 393 Apr 11 10:22 telnet.xml

The file you are looking for is **telnet.xml** file which has the following content:

```
# cat telnet.xml
<?xml version="1.0" encoding="utf-8"?>
<service>
  <short>Telnet</short>
  <description>Telnet is a protocol for logging into remote machines. It is
unencrypted, and provides little security from network snooping attacks.
Enabling telnet is not recommended. You need the telnet-server package installed
for this option to be useful.</description>
  <port port="23" protocol="tcp"/>
</service>
```

As you see, it provides information about the telnet program, the port it uses (23) and the protocol type which is TCP (Transmission Control Protocol).

Step 5:

This step involves adding the service in the Firewalld "allow" list. In step 3, we stopped the Firewalld daemon. It's time to start it again and add the telnet service.

Start the Firewalld:

```
# systemctl restart firewalld
```

Add the service telnet to the Firewalld "Allow" list:

 # firewall-cmd --add-service=telnet

success

Note that the response from the system is "success." Since we have only public zone as default; we need not specify the zone. In case, you decide to have multiple zones in your environment, you would have to specify to which zone **telnet** service is being added, so the alternative command is

 # firewall-cmd –zone=public --add-service=telnet

Check if the service telnet has been added using the following command:

 # firewall-cmd --list-services

ssh dhcpv6-client telnet

Yes, it is a success, **telnet** is now on the list.

You should be able to **telnet** from Windows 10 system with Centos Firewalld on and your system in the secure state. This is the desired state. Shutdown the Firewalld only to troubleshoot.

However, the above commands apply to the current session only, to make it a perpetual setting, use the **-permanent** flag as shown in the following command:

#firewall-cmd --permanent --add-service=telnet

Up till now, you have learned how to configure Linux Services into the Firewalld list, but the point is that software vendors also use TCP ports for communication. There is a wide variety of applications available on the market. A server-end of the application is installed on the Server machine. The Server machine is a misnomer, with powerful CPUs, even your ordinary desktop system can be a "**server**." The point is that the Server serves services which the client-end applications use, it could be database entries, authentication and security services or a mind-boggling number of services in many business verticals. The client-end application could be on a Linux Machine or Windows, it does not matter, because the mode of communication is TCP/IP. Even the Server-end part of the application can reside on any Operating System if it has the TCP/IP stack installed.

The client-end application sends a request to the server-end application, and if certain algorithms and security parameters are fulfilled, the request is granted by the server-end application.

How does the client-end application know the server?

An environment variable is set in the user's environment that points to the name of the server or its IP address and the port at which the Server-end application is waiting for the client request. The Port is either a TCP or UDP port. It is a unique number associated with the server-end application. Remember it is only unique to the machine. Imagine, a hotel with room numbers, if Lisa is staying at room number 420 and Jeff is staying at room number 840, and you have a bouquet for Jeff, understandably if you go to Lisa's room, the result may not be fortuitous for you.

Similarly, think of the port number as the virtual counterpart of a room number, the client-end application must know the CORRECT port number for the services it seeks. One way is setting an environment variable, for example, for a Squid Proxy Server, you set a variable called **http_proxy**, and now the browsers look at the VALUE of **http_proxy** for Internet connectivity. If the server-end of the proxy server is down or the port the proxy uses is blocked by the firewall, the client-end application, in this case, browsers, cannot access the Internet.

Setting the **http_proxy** environment variable on a client Linux Box:

$ export http_proxy=3128@192.168.1.8

Secondly, during the client-end configuration step, the setup program asks you the IP address or hostname of the server-end application and the port addresses it listens for the client requests. Please note, the name and vendor of the software applications may change, but the principles are SAME or SIMILAR.

Step 1:

What is a Proxy Server?

A proxy server is an in-between system between your computer and the Internet.

What are the features of a Proxy Server?

- Acts as a Tunnel proxy
- Access Control List support
- Stops "bad" websites
- Logging

How to install a proxy server?

Login as root and issue the following command:

 # yum install squid

We are going to install the Proxy server on the system, **bobby**, whose IP address is 192.168.1.8. The system also has the Firewalld installed.

Step 2

You have installed squid proxy server.

In Linux, configuration files relating to services and daemons are in the **/etc** directory. Such files have .**conf** as their extension. Squid configuration files are no exception and exist in the **/etc/squid** directory.

The name of the Squid Configuration file is **squid.conf.**

Step 3

Find the port that Squid Proxy Server uses by default, the information is available in the **squid.conf** file.

Navigate to the **/etc/squid** directory and open **squid.conf** file

```
# Squid normally listens to port 3128
http_port 3128
```

In the real world, system administrators change this port to 8080. In this example, let it listen at 3128, but you can go ahead make the change to 8080 in **squid.conf** file and save it.

Step 4

Using the **firewall-cmd** command to gain the same information as in the previous step. It is interesting to see if the **firewall-cmd** command lists the squid service, let's check using **firewall-cmd –get-services** command:

```
[root@bobby squid]# firewall-cmd --get-services | grep squid
RH-Satellite-6 amanda-client amanda-k5-client bacula bacula-client bitcoin bitcoin-
rpc bitcoin-testnet bitcoin-testnet-rpc ceph ceph-mon cfengine condor-collector ctd
b dhcp dhcpv6 dhcpv6-client dns docker-registry dropbox-lansync elasticsearch freei
pa-ldap freeipa-ldaps freeipa-replication freeipa-trust ftp ganglia-client ganglia-
master high-availability http https imap imaps ipp ipp-client ipsec iscsi-target ka
dmin kerberos kibana klogin kpasswd kshell ldap ldaps libvirt libvirt-tls managesie
ve mdns mosh mountd ms-wbt mssql mysql nfs nfs3 nrpe ntp openvpn ovirt-imageio ovir
t-storageconsole ovirt-vmconsole pmcd pmproxy pmwebapi pmwebapis pop3 pop3s postgre
sql privoxy proxy-dhcp ptp pulseaudio puppetmaster quassel radius rpc-bind rsh rsyn
cd samba samba-client sane sip sips smtp smtp-submission smtps snmp snmptrap spider
oak-lansync squid ssh synergy syslog syslog-tls telnet tftp tftp-client tinc tor-so
cks transmission-client vdsm vnc-server wbem-https xmpp-bosh xmpp-client xmpp-local
 xmpp-server
```

Step 5

Starting the Squid Service on bobby, 192.168.1.8.

 # service squid start
Redirecting to /bin/systemctl start squid.service

To check if the Squid Server Service is running issue the following command

 # service squid status

```
[root@bobby squid]# service squid status
Redirecting to /bin/systemctl status squid.service
● squid.service - Squid caching proxy
   Loaded: loaded (/usr/lib/systemd/system/squid.service; disabled; vendor preset:
disabled)
   Active: active (running) since Sun 2018-09-09 15:18:24 IST; 1min 23s ago
  Process: 16846 ExecStart=/usr/sbin/squid $SQUID_OPTS -f $SQUID_CONF (code=exited,
status=0/SUCCESS)
  Process: 16841 ExecStartPre=/usr/libexec/squid/cache_swap.sh (code=exited, status
=0/SUCCESS)
 Main PID: 16849 (squid)
   CGroup: /system.slice/squid.service
           ├─16849 /usr/sbin/squid -f /etc/squid/squid.conf
           ├─16851 (squid-1) -f /etc/squid/squid.conf
           └─16852 (logfile-daemon) /var/log/squid/access.log

Sep 09 15:18:24 bobby systemd[1]: Starting Squid caching proxy...
Sep 09 15:18:24 bobby systemd[1]: Started Squid caching proxy.
Sep 09 15:18:24 bobby squid[16849]: Squid Parent: will start 1 kids
Sep 09 15:18:24 bobby squid[16849]: Squid Parent: (squid-1) process 16851 started
```

Step 6

Check the port Squid Server Service is running, you need this information to open the port in the Firewalld list.

```
[root@bobby squid]# netstat -plant | grep squid
tcp6        0        0 :::3128              :::*                LISTEN        168
51/(squid-1)
```

So, you have now the confirmation by using the **netstat -plant** command that squid is running on TCP port 3128 with PID 16851.

Step 7:

You can, of course, add the service **squid**, but here we are simulating how to add a port for a third-party software application.

Adding the port 3128

 # firewall-cmd --zone=public --add-port=3128/tcp
success

Checking if the port is added in the Firewalld list

 # firewall-cmd --zone=public --list-ports
3128/tcp

Step 8:

The clients who have set the **http_proxy** environment variable to 3128@192.168.1.8 on their systems should be able to connect to the Internet from the Squid Proxy Server service running on hostname, **bobby**.

Do not forget that services that run on TCP/IP are not dependent upon the Operating System you use. Thus, you can use Windows 10 platform to troubleshoot Firewalld issues, this chapter is connected to the previous chapter, as we troubleshoot if the Port 3128 used by the Squid Proxy Server on Centos machine is blocked or not. One of the most dependable tools I have come across in my quarter-century of IT experience has to be that nifty free tool from Microsoft called **portqry**. It has indeed saved me from many an irate customer who would NOT believe that a certain port is blocked at their end and because of which the client-end software is not working.

Though not a fan of GUI tools, I do like the GUI interface of portqry, which you can download from the following location:

http://download.microsoft.com/download/3/f/4/3f4c6a54-65f0-4164-bdec-a3411ba24d3a/PortQryUI.exe

Step 1

Gathering information

Problem statement	Internet not working
IP address of the client:	192.168.1.10
IP address of the system where the proxy server is running	192.168.1.8
Hostname of the system where Squid Server is running	Bobby
Is the Squid Proxy Server Service running?	Yes, the system was down due to hardware failure and the Network engineer has started the Squid Proxy Server
Which port is the Squid Proxy server running on bobby (192.168.1.8)?	The default port 3128
What kind of service is it? TCP or UDP?	TCP

Step 2

Check connectivity from 192.168.1.10 to the system where proxy Server is running, which is 192.168.1.8 using the ping command:

```
[client_user@sujata ~]$ ping 192.168.1.8
PING 192.168.1.8 (192.168.1.8) 56(84) bytes of data.
64 bytes from 192.168.1.8: icmp_seq=1 ttl=64 time=0.429 ms
64 bytes from 192.168.1.8: icmp_seq=2 ttl=64 time=1.48 ms
64 bytes from 192.168.1.8: icmp_seq=3 ttl=64 time=0.463 ms
64 bytes from 192.168.1.8: icmp_seq=4 ttl=64 time=1.30 ms
64 bytes from 192.168.1.8: icmp_seq=5 ttl=64 time=0.455 ms
64 bytes from 192.168.1.8: icmp_seq=6 ttl=64 time=0.398 ms
64 bytes from 192.168.1.8: icmp_seq=7 ttl=64 time=0.463 ms
```

Connectivity is fine between the client and the Server, yet the Internet is now running.

Step 3:

You decide to investigate this issue from your Windows 10 machine. Your IP address also belongs to the same Network subnet.

Ping test

You can ping from your Windows machine to the Squid Server 192.168.1.8

Telnet test

While you can telnet to 192.168.1.8 from the Windows machine. You may conclude that the port 23 is not blocked, you can also use telnet to troubleshoot if Squid Server port is open or not by forcing telnet to use 3128 instead of its default port.

```
C:\>telnet 192.168.1.8 3128
Connecting To 192.168.1.8...Could not open connection to the host, on port 3128: C
onnect failed
```

You now suspect that there is something wrong with the port 3128 when you use telnet.

Step 4:

You decide to perform the last test with portqry because it is the most reliable that is available on the Windows platform (among free tools).

The Portqry test has three modes for reporting the status of the TCP or UDP port, they are

Listening	Means the port is not blocked by the firewall of the remote machine
Not Listening	Means that no service or daemon is using the port for client requests on the remote machine.
Filtered	Indicates that the port is filtered on the remote machine and needs to be opened by the Network or System Admin responsible for the remote machine.

Invoke the **portqueryui.exe** utility from the default path **c:\PortQryUI**

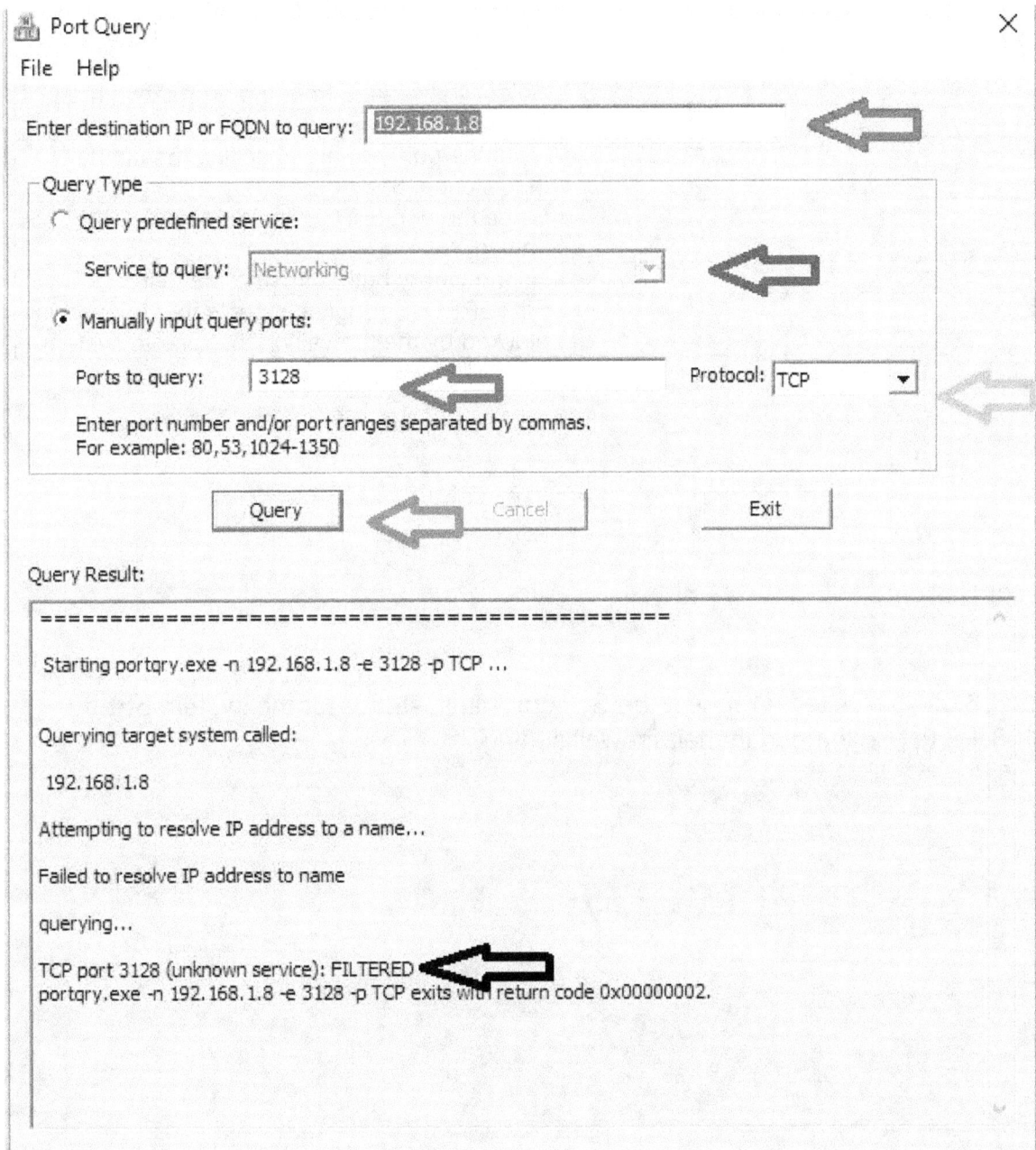

Refer to the following table to understand what the colored arrows stand for:

Arrow Color	Actions/Results
Red	Input the IP address of the Remote system whose port you are checking, in this case, it is 192.168.1.8
Blue	Select Networking from the drop-down menu for Query Type
Purple	Input the port you are checking the status of, in this case, 3128.
Pink	Since the port is TCP, leave the default setting
Brown	Hit the Query button to start the test
Black	FILTERED: Strongly suggests that the port is blocked by the firewall on the remote system.

Step 5:

Your conclusion:

The port 3128 is blocked, I request the System Administrator for the system **bobby**, 192.168.1.8 to add the port in their firewall setting.

Step 6:

You have received word from the System Administrator responsible for bobby, 192.168.1.8, that she has added the port 3128 in the Firewalld list. To close the ticket from your end, run the portqry software again and verify that the port is indeed open.

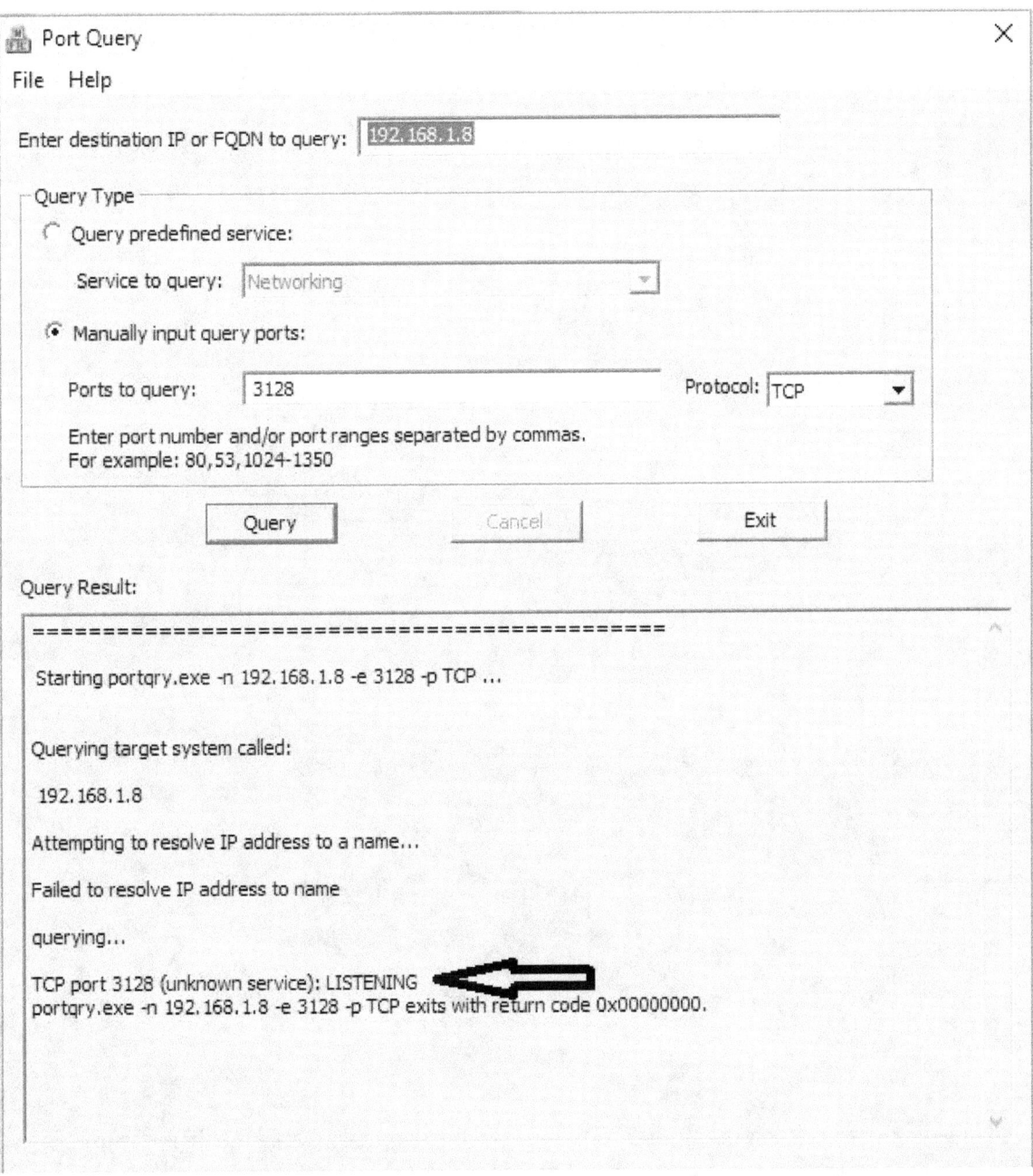

You can close the ticket as you see that the port 3128 is in the Listening mode.

In today's digital age, cybersecurity has become more important than ever before. Hackers and cybercriminals are always on the lookout for vulnerabilities to exploit, and businesses need to take proactive measures to protect their networks and data. One of the best ways to do this is by setting up a multi-zone firewall. In this chapter, we will discuss how to set up a multi-zone firewall in firewalld.

Before we dive into setting up a multi-zone firewall in Firewalld, let's first understand again what zones are. A zone is a collection of network connections that have similar security requirements. Each zone has its own set of firewall rules and policies. Firewalld comes with a set of predefined zones such as public, internal, external, and dmz. You can also create custom zones based on your specific needs.

Step 1: Create the Zones

The first step in setting up a multi-zone firewall is to create the zones. In this example, we will create two custom zones: internal and external.

To create a zone, use the following command (login as root or use sudo):

firewall-cmd --permanent --new-zone=<zone_name>

For example, to create the internal zone, use the following command:

firewall-cmd --permanent --new-zone=internal

Similarly, to create the external zone, use the following command:

firewall-cmd --permanent --new-zone=external

Step 2: Define the Interfaces

The next step is to define the interfaces that belong to each zone. In this example, we will assume that eth0 is the internal interface and eth1 is the external interface.

To add an interface to a zone, use the following command:

firewall-cmd --permanent --zone=<zone_name> --add-interface=<interface_name>

For example, to add eth0 to the internal zone, use the following command:

firewall-cmd --permanent --zone=internal --add-interface=eth0

Similarly, to add eth1 to the external zone, use the following command:

firewall-cmd --permanent --zone=external --add-interface=eth1

Step 3: Define the Firewall Rules

The final step is to define the firewall rules for each zone. In this example, we will allow HTTP and HTTPS traffic from the external zone to the internal zone.

To allow HTTP traffic, use the following command:

firewall-cmd --permanent --zone=internal --add-service=http

To allow HTTPS traffic, use the following command:

firewall-cmd --permanent --zone=internal --add-service=https

Step 4: Reload the Firewall Configuration

After defining the zones and rules, you need to reload the firewall configuration for the changes to take effect. Use the following command to reload the firewall configuration:

firewall-cmd --reload

Setting up a multi-zone firewall in FIREWALLD is a simple and effective way to protect your network and data from cyber threats. By creating custom zones, defining interfaces, and setting up firewall rules, you can ensure that your network is secure and protected. With FIREWALLD, you can easily manage your firewall configuration and make changes as needed.

Firewalld is a front-end application that manages iptables rules through the use of zones, services, and ports. Firewalld stores its configuration and rules in XML files, which are located in the /usr/lib/firewalld and /etc/firewalld directories.

In this chapter, you will learn the format of XML configuration files in firewalld, including the syntax, elements, and attributes that are used to define firewall rules and configurations.

Overview of XML Configuration Files

XML (Extensible Markup Language) is a markup language that is used to describe data. It is a standard format for data exchange between different applications and systems. Firewalld uses XML configuration files to store its rules and configurations. XML files consist of elements, attributes, and values. The elements are the building blocks of an XML file, and they define the structure of the data. The attributes provide additional information about the elements, and the values are the data that is stored in the elements.

In firewalld, the XML files are used to define the firewall rules and configurations. Each XML file contains one or more elements that define a specific aspect of the firewall configuration, such as zones, services, ports, or rich rules.

Syntax of XML Configuration Files

The syntax of an XML file is defined by a set of rules that specify how the elements, attributes, and values should be structured. The basic syntax of an XML file consists of the following elements:

```
<?xml version="1.0" encoding="utf-8"?>
<root_element>
  <child_element attribute="value">data</child_element>
</root_element>
```

The <?xml version="1.0" encoding="utf-8"?> declaration specifies the version and encoding of the XML file. The root_element is the top-level element of the XML file, and it contains one or more child elements. The child_element is an example of a child element, and it can have attributes and values.

Elements in XML Configuration Files

In firewalld, the XML files are used to define the firewall rules and configurations. Each XML file contains one or more elements that define a specific aspect of the firewall configuration. The following are the most commonly used elements in firewalld XML configuration files:

1. firewall

The firewall element is the top-level element in firewalld XML configuration files. It contains one or more zone elements, which define the firewall zones.

```
<firewall>
  <zone name="public">
   ...
  </zone>
  <zone name="internal">
   ...
  </zone>
</firewall>
```

2. zone

The zone element defines a firewall zone, which is a set of rules that apply to a specific network zone. It can contain one or more service and port elements, which define the services and ports that are allowed in the zone.

```
<zone name="public">
  <service name="ssh"/>
  <port port="80" protocol="tcp"/>
</zone>
```

3. service

The service element defines a service that is allowed in a firewall zone. It contains the name of the service, which corresponds to a predefined service in the /usr/lib/firewalld/services directory.

```
<service name="ssh"/>
```

4. port

The port element defines a port that is allowed in a firewall zone. It contains the port number and the protocol.

```
<port port="80" protocol="tcp"/>
```

5. source

The source element defines the source address or network that is allowed in a firewall zone.

```
<source address="192.168.1.0/24"/>
```

6. rule

The rule element defines a firewall rule that applies to a specific firewall zone. It can contain one or more source, service, and port elements.

```
<rule family="ipv4">
  <source address="192.168.1.0/24"/>
  <port protocol="tcp" port="80"/>
  <accept/>
</rule>
```

7. rich-rule

The rich-rule element defines a complex firewall rule that applies to a specific firewall zone. It can contain multiple criteria, such as source, destination, service, and port.

```
<rich-rule>
  <family>ipv4</family>
  <source address="192.168.1.0/24"/>
  <destination address="10.0.0.0/24"/>
  <service name="ssh"/>
  <port port="80" protocol="tcp"/>
  <accept/>
</rich-rule>
```

Attributes in XML Configuration Files

In firewalld XML configuration files, each element can have one or more attributes that provide additional information about the element. The following are the most commonly used attributes in firewalld XML configuration files:

1. name

The name attribute specifies the name of the firewall zone, service, or port.

```
<zone name="public">
  ...
</zone>
```

```
<service name="ssh">
  ...
</service>

<port port="80" protocol="tcp">
  ...
</port>
```

2. address

The address attribute specifies the IP address or network that is allowed in the firewall zone.

```
<source address="192.168.1.0/24"/>
```

3. protocol

The protocol attribute specifies the protocol that is allowed in the firewall zone.

```
<port port="80" protocol="tcp"/>
```

4. port

The port attribute specifies the port number that is allowed in the firewall zone.

```
<port port="80" protocol="tcp"/>
```

5. family

The family attribute specifies the IP version that is allowed in the firewall zone.

```
<rich-rule family="ipv4">
  ...
</rich-rule>
```

6. action

The action attribute specifies the action that is taken when a rule is matched.

```
<rule>
  ...
  <accept/>
</rule>
```

Firewalld uses XML configuration files to store its rules and configurations. The XML files consist of elements, attributes, and values, which define the structure of the data. The most commonly used elements in firewalld XML configuration files are firewall, zone, service, port, source, rule, and rich-rule. The most commonly used attributes are name, address, protocol, port, family, and action. Understanding the format of XML configuration files in firewalld is essential for managing and configuring firewalls on Linux system

Firewalld is a dynamic firewall management tool that provides a flexible way to configure the firewall rules. It uses a concept of zones to define the level of trust of network connections. By default, firewalld comes with a set of predefined rules for common services, but the real power of firewalld lies in its ability to create custom rules using rich rules.

Rich rules are a powerful feature that allows you to create complex firewall rules beyond the basic rules. In this chapter, we will discuss how to use rich rules in firewalld to create custom firewall rules.

Rich rules are a way to create custom firewall rules that are more complex than the basic rules that come with firewalld. Rich rules use a rich language to define rules that can match on multiple criteria, including source and destination IP addresses, source and destination ports, protocols, and more.

Rich rules are defined in XML format, which can be loaded into firewalld using the --add-rich-rule option. The rich language is well-documented, and firewalld provides a set of predefined rich rules that you can use as a starting point for creating your own rules.

Creating Rich Rules

To create a rich rule, you need to define the rule in XML format and load it into firewalld using the --add-rich-rule option. Below is an example of a simple rich rule that allows incoming traffic on port 80:

```xml
<?xml version="1.0" encoding="utf-8"?>
<rule>
 <family>ipv4</family>
 <source address="192.168.1.0/24"/>
 <service name="http"/>
 <accept/>
</rule>
```

In this example, the rule matches incoming traffic from the subnet 192.168.1.0/24 on port 80 and accepts the traffic.

You can create more complex rules by combining multiple criteria. For example, the following rule matches incoming traffic from the subnet 192.168.1.0/24 on port 80 and 443 and accepts the traffic:

```xml
<?xml version="1.0" encoding="utf-8"?>
<rule>
 <family>ipv4</family>
 <source address="192.168.1.0/24"/>
 <port protocol="tcp" port="80,443"/>
 <accept/>
</rule>
```

Loading Rich Rules

Once you have defined a rich rule, you can load it into firewalld using the --add-rich-rule option. For example, to load the simple rich rule that allows incoming traffic on port 80, use the following command:

```
firewall-cmd --zone=public --add-rich-rule='rule family="ipv4" source address="192.168.1.0/24" service name="http" accept'
```

Similarly, to load the more complex rich rule that allows incoming traffic on ports 80 and 443, use the following command:

```
firewall-cmd --zone=public --add-rich-rule='rule family="ipv4" source address="192.168.1.0/24" port protocol="tcp" port="80,443" accept'
```

Rich rules are a powerful feature of firewalld that allows you to create custom firewall rules beyond the basic rules. By defining rules in XML format and loading them into firewalld using the --add-rich-rule option, you can create complex rules that match on multiple criteria. Rich rules provide a flexible way to configure the firewall rules and help you to better protect your network from cyber threats.

Firewalld is a powerful firewall management tool that provides a lot of functionality out of the box. However, there may be times when the default rules and configurations are not enough to meet your needs. In these cases, you may need to create direct rules, which allow you to add custom rules directly to the iptables ruleset used by Firewalld.

Direct rules give you a lot of flexibility and control over the firewall configuration, but they can also be more complex and difficult to manage than the standard firewalld rules. In this chapter, we will explore the advanced configuration options available through direct rules on Firewalld.

What are Direct Rules?

Direct rules are custom iptables rules that are added directly to the underlying iptables ruleset. These rules are not managed by the firewalld daemon, and they are not subject to the same management and configuration options as the standard firewalld rules. Instead, direct rules are added to the iptables ruleset and are managed directly by the iptables command.

There are several different types of direct rules that can be used with Firewalld, including:

Raw Rules: Raw rules are custom iptables rules that are added directly to the raw table of the iptables ruleset. These rules provide low-level packet filtering capabilities, but they can be more complex and difficult to manage than other types of direct rules.

Filter Rules: Filter rules are custom iptables rules that are added directly to the filter table of the iptables ruleset. These rules provide packet filtering capabilities at the network layer, and they are commonly used to block or allow specific types of traffic.

NAT Rules: NAT rules are custom iptables rules that are added directly to the NAT table of the iptables ruleset. These rules are used to modify the source or destination addresses of network packets, and they are commonly used to implement port forwarding or masquerading.

How to Create Direct Rules

Creating direct rules in Firewalld is a two-step process. First, you need to create a custom rule file that defines the iptables rule you want to add to the ruleset. Then, you need to add the custom rule file to the firewalld configuration directory so that it will be loaded when the firewall is started.

Creating a Custom Rule File

To create a custom rule file, you need to create a new file in the /etc/firewalld/directories directory with a name that ends in **.rule**. For example, if you wanted to create a filter rule that blocks all traffic to a specific IP address, you could create a file named **block-ip.rule** with the following content:

-A INPUT -s 192.168.1.100 -j DROP

This rule would add a filter rule to the INPUT chain of the iptables ruleset that drops all traffic from the IP address 192.168.1.100.

Adding the Rule File to the Configuration Directory

Once you have created your custom rule file, you need to add it to the firewalld configuration directory so that it will be loaded when the firewall is started. To do this, you can use the following command:

cp block-ip.rule /etc/firewalld/directories/

This command will copy the block-ip.rule file to the /etc/firewalld/directories directory, which is where Firewalld looks for custom rule files.

Managing Direct Rules

Managing direct rules can be more complex than managing the standard firewalld rules, since direct rules are not managed by the firewalld daemon. However, there are several tools and commands that can be used to manage direct rules.

The iptables Command

The iptables command is the primary tool used to manage the iptables ruleset, including direct rules. You can use the iptables command to view, add, modify, or delete direct rules from the iptables ruleset. For example, to view all of the direct rules in the iptables ruleset, you can use the following command:

iptables -L -n -v

This command will list all of the rules in the iptables ruleset, including any direct rules that have been added.

The firewalld Command

The firewalld command can also be used to manage direct rules, although it provides a more limited set of options than the iptables command. You can use the firewalld command to view the status of the firewall, reload the firewall configuration, or add or remove direct rules from the configuration directory.

For example, to reload the firewalld configuration after adding a new direct rule file, you can use the following command:

firewall-cmd --reload

This command will reload the firewalld configuration, causing any new direct rule files to be loaded into the iptables ruleset.

Direct rules provide a powerful way to customize the firewall configuration in Firewalld. With direct rules, you can add custom iptables rules directly to the iptables ruleset, giving you more flexibility and control over the firewall configuration. However, direct rules can also be more complex and difficult to manage than the standard firewalld rules, so it is important to use them with care and to have a good understanding of iptables and the underlying network configuration.

Firewalld provides extensive logging options, allowing you to log firewall events to a variety of destinations, including files, syslog servers, and remote log servers. Logging can be configured at both the firewall level and the rule level, giving you fine-grained control over which events are logged and where they are logged.

Configuring Firewall Logging

To enable logging for the entire firewall, you can use the firewall-cmd command to add the --log-denied option to the firewall configuration:

firewall-cmd --set-log-denied=all

This will enable logging for all denied packets, which can be useful for troubleshooting network connectivity issues.

You can also configure the log level for the firewall using the --log-level option. The log level can be set to one of the following values:

- emergency

- alert

- critical

- error

- warning

- notice

- info

- debug

For example, to set the log level to notice, you can use the following command:

firewall-cmd --set-log-level=notice

This will configure the firewall to log events at the notice level and above.

Configuring Rule Logging

In addition to logging at the firewall level, you can also configure logging for individual rules using the --log-prefix and --log-level options. These options allow you to specify a custom log prefix and log level for each rule.

For example, to configure logging for a rule that blocks incoming traffic on port 22, you can use the following command:

firewall-cmd --add-rich-rule='rule family="ipv4" source address="192.168.1.0/24" port port="22" protocol="tcp" reject log prefix="SSH BLOCKED" level="info"'

This command will add a rule that blocks incoming traffic on port 22 from the 192.168.1.0/24 network and logs the event with the prefix "SSH BLOCKED" and log level "info".

Viewing Firewall Logs

Once logging is enabled, firewall events can be viewed in a variety of ways. The most common way to view firewall logs is to use the journalctl command to view the system journal:

journalctl -u firewalld

You should see something like the following snapshot:

```
-- Logs begin at Sat 2023-03-04 22:48:58 IST, end at Sat 2023-03-11 21:46:35 IST. -
Mar 04 22:49:05 sujata systemd[1]: Starting firewalld - dynamic firewall daemon...
Mar 04 22:49:06 sujata systemd[1]: Started firewalld - dynamic firewall daemon.
Mar 04 22:49:07 sujata firewalld[683]: WARNING: AllowZoneDrifting is enabled. This
```

This command will display all log entries generated by the Firewalld service. You can filter the output by date, time, and other criteria using the journalctl options.

You can also configure Firewalld to log events to a file by adding the --log-file option to the firewall configuration:

firewall-cmd --set-log-file=/var/log/firewalld.log

This will configure Firewalld to log events to the /var/log/firewalld.log file, which can be viewed using a text editor or other file viewer.

We will end the books with the following sub-topics:

Masquerading and NAT in firewalld

Masquerading and NAT are two essential features of firewalld that enable you to manage network traffic and protect your system from malicious attacks. Masquerading is used to hide private IP addresses behind public IP addresses, while NAT is used to map one IP address to another. In this chapter, we'll go over the basics of masquerading and NAT, how to configure them using firewalld, and provide several examples to help you understand how to use them in different scenarios.

What is Masquerading?

Masquerading is the process of hiding a private IP address behind a public IP address, allowing you to share a single public IP address among several devices on a local network. This is particularly useful for networks that don't have enough public IP addresses to assign to each device. With masquerading, all the devices on your local network share a single public IP address, which is then used to communicate with devices outside of your network.

What is NAT?

NAT (Network Address Translation) is the process of mapping one IP address to another. NAT is commonly used to facilitate communication between devices on different networks. NAT is used to translate private IP addresses to public IP addresses, allowing devices on a private network to communicate with devices on a public network. NAT can also be used to translate public IP addresses to private IP addresses, allowing devices on a public network to communicate with devices on a private network.

How to Configure Masquerading and NAT using firewalld

Firewalld provides an easy way to configure masquerading and NAT using the masquerade and forward options respectively. To enable masquerading, you need to add the masquerade option to the zone where your network interface is located. For example, if your network interface is located in the public zone, you can enable masquerading by running the following command:

firewall-cmd --zone=public --add-masquerade

This command will add the masquerade option to the public zone, allowing devices on your local network to access the internet using the public IP address.

To enable NAT, you need to add the forward option to the zone where your network interface is located. For example, if your network interface is located in the public zone, you can enable NAT by running the following command:

```
firewall-cmd --zone=public --add-forward-port=port=80:proto=tcp:toaddr=192.168.1.2:toport=80
```

This command will add a NAT rule that forwards all traffic received on port 80 on the public IP address to port 80 on the private IP address 192.168.1.2. In this example, the port option specifies the source port (i.e., the port on the firewall), proto specifies the protocol, toaddr specifies the IP address of the destination server, and toport specifies the destination port.

Make sure to replace the IP address and port numbers with the actual values for your environment.

Examples of Masquerading and NAT in firewalld

Let's look at a few examples of how masquerading and NAT can be used in different scenarios.

Example 1: Masquerading for a Simple Home Network

Suppose you have a simple home network with several devices connected to a router. The router is connected to the internet using a single public IP address. To enable masquerading, you need to add the masquerade option to the zone where your network interface is located. In this case, let's assume that your network interface is located in the public zone. To enable masquerading, you can run the following command:

firewall-cmd --zone=public --add-masquerade

Once masquerading is enabled, all the devices on your local network can access the internet using the public IP address.

Example 2: NAT for a Web Server

Suppose you have a web server located on a private network with a private IP address of 192.168.1.2. You want to make the web server accessible from the internet using a public IP address. To do this, you need to configure NAT on your firewall. In this case, let's assume that your network interface is located in the public zone. To enable NAT, you can run the following command:

firewall-cmd --zone=public --add-forward-port=port=80:proto=tcp:toaddr=192.168.1.2:toport=80

This command will add a NAT rule that forwards all traffic received on port 80 on the public IP address to port 80 on the private IP address 192.168.1.2.

Example 3: NAT for a Mail Server

Suppose you have a mail server located on a private network with a private IP address of 192.168.1.3. You want to make the mail server accessible from the internet using a public IP address. To do this, you need to configure NAT on your firewall. In this case, let's assume that your network interface is located in the public zone. To enable NAT, you can run the following command:

firewall-cmd --zone=public --add-forward-port=port=25:proto=tcp:toaddr=192.168.1.3:toport=25

This command will add a NAT rule that forwards all traffic received on port 25 on the public IP address to port 25 on the private IP address 192.168.1.3.

Masquerading and NAT are two important features of firewalld that allow you to manage network traffic and protect your system from malicious attacks. Masquerading is used to hide private IP addresses behind public IP addresses, while NAT is used to map one IP address to another. With firewalld, you can easily configure masquerading and NAT using the masquerade and forward options respectively. By understanding how to use these features, you can enhance the security of your network and make your devices accessible from the internet.

IPset in firewalld

Firewalld is a dynamic firewall management tool that allows administrators to manage the network traffic by defining rules, zones, and services. It is the default firewall configuration tool in many Linux distributions such as CentOS, Fedora, and Red Hat Enterprise Linux.

One of the features of firewalld is the support for IPsets. An IPset is a set of IP addresses, networks, and ports that can be matched against incoming or outgoing traffic. IPsets can simplify firewall rules by grouping multiple IP addresses and networks into a single set, making it easier to manage firewall policies.

Creating IPsets

To create an IPset in firewalld, you can use the --new-Ipset option followed by the name of the new IPset, the type of IPset, and the family of the IP addresses to be used. For example, to create a new IPset named myipset with the type hash:ip and the family inet, you can run the following command:

firewall-cmd --permanent --new-ipset=myipset --type=hash:ip --option=family=inet

This command creates a new IPset of type hash:ip that uses the IPv4 address family. You can also create an IPset that uses the IPv6 address family by changing the family option to inet6.

Adding IP addresses to IPsets

Once you have created an IPset, you can add IP addresses and networks to it using the --add-entry option followed by the name of the IPset and the IP address or network to be added. For example, to add the IP address 10.0.0.1 to the myipset IPset, you can run the following command:

firewall-cmd --permanent --ipset=myipset --add-entry=10.0.0.1

You can also add a network to the IPset by specifying the network address and the subnet mask. For example, to add the network 192.168.0.0/24 to the myipset IPset, you can run the following command:

firewall-cmd --permanent --ipset=myipset --add-entry=192.168.0.0/24

Using IPsets in firewall rules

Once you have created an IPset and added IP addresses and networks to it, you can use it in firewall rules to filter incoming or outgoing traffic. To use an IPset in a firewall rule, you can specify the --match-set option followed by the name of the IPset and the direction of the traffic. For example, to allow incoming traffic from the IP addresses and networks in the myipset IPset, you can run the following command:

firewall-cmd --permanent --zone=public --add-rich-rule='rule family=ipv4 source match-set=myipset src accept

This command adds a rich rule to the public zone that allows incoming traffic from the IP addresses and networks in the myipset IPset. You can also use the --match-set option in other directions, such as dst for outgoing traffic.

The last command may error out in some Linux distributions with invalid rule error.

The error message "INVALID_RULE: bad attribute 'match-set'" indicates that the firewall-cmd command is trying to use an invalid or unsupported attribute (match-set) in the --add-rich-rule option.

match-set is a valid attribute in the ipset module, which allows you to define a set of IP addresses and/or network ranges that can be used in firewall rules. However, it is not supported in the firewalld rich rule syntax used by firewall-cmd.

To allow traffic from a set of IP addresses defined in an ipset set, you can use the following firewall-cmd command:

firewall-cmd --permanent --zone=public --add-rich-rule='rule family=ipv4 source ipset=myipset accept'

In this command, ipset=myipset specifies the name of the ipset set containing the allowed IP addresses. You would need to create and populate the myipset set with the desired IP addresses before using this rule.

Make sure to replace myipset with the actual name of your ipset set.

IPsets are a powerful feature of firewalld that can simplify firewall rules by grouping multiple IP addresses and networks into a single set. By using IPsets, administrators can easily manage firewall policies and improve the security of their networks.

Fail2Ban is an open-source intrusion prevention software that is widely used to protect servers from brute force attacks, DOS attacks, and other types of malicious activities. It works by monitoring log files and detecting suspicious activity and then blocking the IP addresses of the attackers.

Firewalld is a dynamic firewall management tool that is used to manage network traffic. It is a default firewall in most Linux distributions and provides a flexible and powerful way to control network traffic on a Linux system. In this topic, we will discuss the integration of Fail2Ban with firewalld.

Installing Fail2Ban

Before we proceed with the integration, we need to install Fail2Ban on our system. Fail2Ban is available in the default repositories of most Linux distributions, and you can install it using the package manager of your distribution.

For example, on a Debian-based system, you can install Fail2Ban using the following command:

sudo apt-get install fail2ban

Similarly, on a Red Hat-based system, you can install it using the following command:

yum install epel-release

yum install fail2ban

Note: If you install fail2ban before epil-release, you will get an error.

Once you have installed Fail2Ban, the next step is to configure it to work with firewalld. By default, Fail2Ban comes with a configuration file located at /etc/fail2ban/jail.conf. You can edit this file to configure Fail2Ban according to your requirements.

To configure Fail2Ban to work with firewalld, you need to specify the backend in the configuration file. The backend specifies the firewall software that Fail2Ban will use to block IP addresses. In our case, we want to use firewalld as the backend. To do this, open the configuration file in a text editor and add the following line:

backend = systemd

Just use the command as root

echo 'backend = systemd' >> /etc/fail2ban/jail.conf

This line specifies that Fail2Ban should use systemd as the backend. Systemd is the init system used by most modern Linux distributions and is required for firewalld to work properly.

Creating a Fail2Ban Jail

After configuring Fail2Ban to use firewalld as the backend, the next step is to create a Fail2Ban jail. A jail is a collection of rules that Fail2Ban uses to monitor the log files and block IP addresses that exhibit suspicious activity.

To create a jail, open the configuration file in a text editor and add the following lines:

```
[firewalld]
enabled = true
filter = firewalld
banaction = firewallcmd-ipset
backend = systemd
```

The above lines create a jail named firewalld and specify the following options:

enabled: This option specifies whether the jail is enabled or not. Set it to true to enable the jail.

filter: This option specifies the filter to be used by the jail. In our case, we want to use the firewalld filter, which is included with Fail2Ban.

banaction: This option specifies the action to be taken when an IP address is blocked. In our case, we want to use the firewallcmd-ipset action, which is a Fail2Ban action that blocks IP addresses using firewalld.

Testing Fail2Ban Integration

Once you have created the jail, you can test the integration by simulating an attack on your system. To do this, you can use the fail2ban-regex command to test the firewalld filter.

For example, to simulate an SSH brute force attack, you can use the following command:

fail2ban-regex /var/log/secure /etc/fail2ban/filter.d/sshd.conf

This command will parse the /var/log/secure log file using the sshd filter and display the IP addresses that match the filter.

Here's what each part of the command does:

fail2ban-regex is the name of the fail2ban utility that we want to run.

/var/log/secure is the path to the log file that we want to test.

/etc/fail2ban/filter.d/sshd.conf is the path to the fail2ban filter that we want to use to test the log file.

By running this command, we are telling fail2ban to use the sshd.conf filter to analyze the /var/log/secure log file and look for authentication failures.

If you are experiencing any issues with the command, make sure that the paths to the log file and filter are correct, and that you have the necessary permissions to access them.

If everything is configured correctly, Fail2Ban should block the IP addresses using firewalld. You can verify this by checking the firewalld rules using the firewall-cmd command.

In this topic, we discussed the integration of Fail2Ban with firewalld. Fail2Ban is a powerful intrusion prevention software that can be used to protect servers from malicious activities, and firewalld is a flexible and powerful tool that can be used to manage network traffic. By integrating Fail2Ban with firewalld, you can enhance the security of your system and protect it from various types of attacks.

www.ingramcontent.com/pod-product-compliance
Lightning Source LLC
Chambersburg PA
CBHW081535220526
45467CB00010B/3203